Shoreham Fort
A Hidden History | Introdu

Shoreham Fort was built in 1857 when the threat of a French invasion was high. As a prototype fortification to the Palmerston Forts, Shoreham incorporated the rectification of earlier design flaws at Littlehampton Fort, built in 1854. Newhaven Lunette Battery was built in 1855 and Shoreham's gun emplacements are of a very similar design but Shoreham is surrounded by a 15ft ditch and a 12ft high wall. These additional features would have posed a major threat to any invading troops.

Palmerston Forts were built around the whole of the United Kingdom to defend our shores and there are very clear examples of Shoreham's design being used. Most notably Fort Nelson, part of the Portsdown Ring in Hampshire.

This book, written by the Friends of Shoreham Fort, will give you an insight in to the Past, Present and Future of Shoreham Fort. You will discover that there is so much more to Shoreham Fort's history, including The Charge of the Light Brigade at Balaclava, Thomas Edison's film cameras, artillery trains and even a famous British actor...

Younger readers will have the added bonus of Jack popping up on some of the pages. Can you help them to spot him...?

Hello...
My name's Jack and you will find me throughout this book. I really hope you recognise me because I have become a master of disguise...

??????????? Why was Shoreham Fort Built?

Since the end of the Napoleonic wars with France in 1815, the state of Britain's defences had seriously declined and it was feared that the nation was once again vulnerable and in the 1850's the threat was coming from France's new emperor, Napoleon III.

Napoleon III, nephew of Napoleon Bonaparte, intended to impose French influence over all of Europe, including Britain. In order to achieve this Napoleon III knew he would have to defeat the British Navy to gain access to the ports in Southern England. It was actually believed that the French would travel across the English Channel, stopping at Shoreham and Littlehampton, before travelling inland to attack our Naval fleet in Portsmouth from behind.

Napoleon III was investing in a new type of warship that was powered by steam, with an armoured plated wooden hull. The new ship 'La Gloire' posed a massive threat to our Navy, as did the fact that France's battle fleet had grown between 1854 and 1858 so that it was equal, in number of ships, to the British Fleet. To combat this threat HMS Warrior was commissioned. Warrior and her sister ship, HMS Black Prince, were the first armour-plated, iron-hulled warships. They were considered to be the fastest, largest and most powerful warships in the world. Britain was once again the ruler of the waves.

Lord Palmerston, Prime Minister at the time, instigated the 'Royal Commission on the Defence of the United Kingdom' in 1859. The sole purpose, to enquire into the ability of the United Kingdom to defend itself against a foreign invasion. In 1860 the Commission's report recommended a huge programme of fortifications to defend the United Kingdom's shores. Based on similar lines to Shoreham Fort, Lord Palmerston initiated the building of numerous forts around the country.

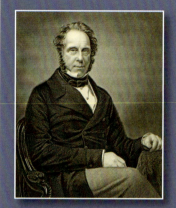

Lord Palmerston was Prime Minister twice, serving 1855~58 and 1859~1865. He was the last prime minister to die in office, two days before his 81st birthday. Palmerston wished to be buried in the new cemetery in Romsey and his grave was actually prepared but Queen Victoria intervened and insisted he was buried in Westminster Abbey. LadyPalmerston was buried with him in 1869.

HMS Warrior was launched 29th December 1860. She was 420ft long with a draught of 26ft 10in and had a maximum speed of 14 knots (16mph). Her armour was 4.5in iron and backed with 18in wood.

Warrior was armed with 26 x smoothbore muzzle-loading 68-pounder cannons; 10 x rifled breechloading 110-pounder cannons and 4 x rifled breech-loading 40-pounder cannons and was manned by 706 officers and enlisted men.

I've been told to keep my eyes open because Napoleon III's new iron clad battleship, La Gloire, is steam driven and doesn't need to rely on the wind, so she's quick... It's a good job that HMS Warrior is being built!

HMS WARRIOR vs LA GLOIRE

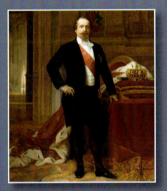

Napoleon III was President of France's Second Republic 1848~1852 and Emperor of the Second French Empire 1852~1870. The disastrous Franco-Prussian War led to his capture at the Battle of Sedan. When peace was arranged between France and Germany he was released and decided to go into exile in England, where he died aged 64.

He was initially buried in St Mary's Church, Chislehurst, before being moved to St. Michael's Abbey, Farnborough, Hampshire in 1888 with his son who had died as a British soldier fighting against the Zulus in South Africa. Napoleon III's wife, Empress Eugénie, was buried in St Michael's Abbey in 1920.

La Gloire was launched 24th November 1859. She was 256ft 8in long with a draught of 27ft 10in and had a maximum speed of 13 knots (15mph). Her armour was 4.7in iron and backed with 17in wood. La Gloire was initially armed with 36 x 6.5in Mle 1858 rifled muzzle-loading cannons and was manned by 570 officers and enlisted men.

HMS Warrior

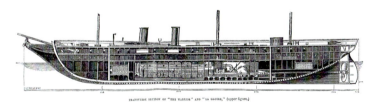

La Gloire

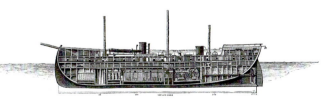

A Hidden History

Littlehampton Gun Battery

Progression of the Forts

Sussex's defences progressed again with a prototype fortification, built at Littlehampton in 1854, which incorporated a perimeter wall. There were many lessons learned about the design issues of this prototype and Shoreham Fort was built in 1857 rectifying them.

Shoreham Fort was actually built to look like an obsolete gun battery, enabling it to become camouflaged with the South Downs behind. This picture, taken a mile out to sea, shows how difficult Shoreham Fort would have been to spot.

One of the early ways to defend the coast was the building of gun batteries. A gun battery consisted of a number of cannons on top of an earthen mound or rampart. Littlehampton Gun Battery, was built in 1759 on the eastern side of Littlehampton Harbour and it held seven cannons. Around 1804 Martello Towers were introduced. The towers only housed one cannon but gave a full 360 degree field of fire. The towers also provided accommodation for one officer and up to twenty five men.

Image Credit - Julian Arnott

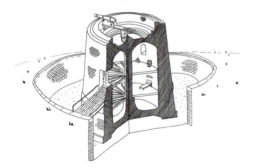

With the illusion of the fort being a gun battery, it would have given the attacking force the false impression that it had old cannon with a very short firing range. The fact that the fort was a trap wouldn't have been discovered until it was too late. The fort's cannons were actually capable of reaching more than four times the distance of the old ones.

Standing up to 40ft high their round structure and thick, solid walls made them very resistant to enemy fire. The height gave the single cannon an advantage in the range it could achieve and some were also surrounded by a defensible ditch. These towers were built to protect us from Napoleon Bonaparte and of those surviving today a great example is found in Seaford, East Sussex which, at time of print, is a museum of Seaford's local history so can be viewed internally and externally.

Being a prototype, Shoreham Fort needed to be built quickly. Due to using lime mortar, work had to stop in the winter months as frost would have caused the lime not to set properly and imperfections would have occurred. Amazingly Shoreham Fort only took six working months to complete.

Fort Nelson

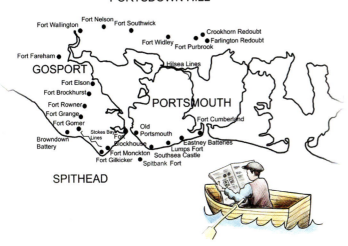

Shoreham Fort's design was elaborated upon to build a whole ring of defences around Portsmouth, known as the Portsdown Ring.

Fort Nelson is one of the Portsdown Ring and is situated on top of Portsdown Hill. Fort Nelson is huge, compared to Shoreham Fort and, although using the same design principles, it took nearly ten years to complete. Work started in 1861, It had its own brick yards on site and required over four million bricks to build, plus tons of field flints too.

Fort Nelson is part of the Royal Armouries. Their collection is extensive, from Imperial cannons to sections of Sadam Hussain's Super Gun. At the time of print there are regular firings, by the Palmerston Fort Society, of various artillery pieces - an experience not be missed.

Napoleon III sent a spy to Shoreham Fort - he saw the design and knew that Lord Palmerston had ordered lots and lots of forts to be built around the country.
He went back to France and told Napoleon III not to chance an attack on England.

A Hidden History

Building & Design | The Barrack Block

Building work began at Shoreham Fort in 1856 and was completed the following June. Details of costs, armaments and accommodation are given in a survey of the fort, drawn up by W. Mumford, Royal Engineers - 1st September 1886. These new plans were done on behalf of the Inspector of General Fortifications and show the original estimated cost was £10,000. The actual cost was £11,685.10s

Barrack blocks were built as living quarters for the soldiers and also for storage. Shoreham Fort's barrack block was split into twelve separate rooms, each having a very specific function.

There is only one entrance to the internal areas of the fort through the barrack block and, with the high carnot wall on the east and west sides, it created a secure perimeter. The entrance passage was protected by a guard room and the external doors were made of heavy oak with plated metal reinforcements. As well as a guard room there was a cell, this would have been used to detain any unauthorised visitors or to discipline any soldiers who broke the rules and regulations.

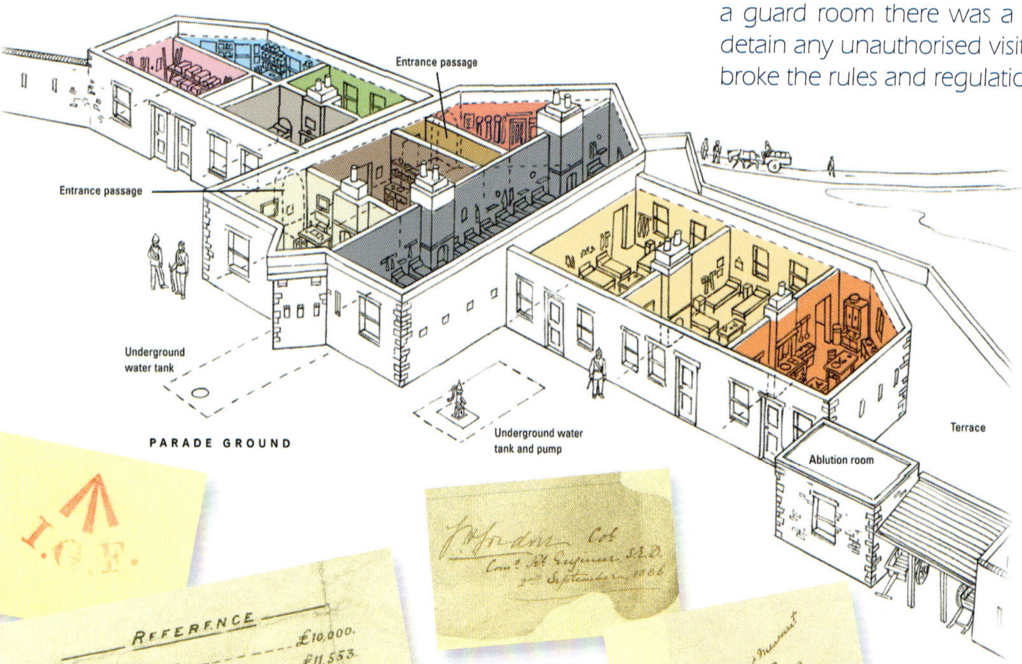

KEY:
- Artillery Store
- Barrack Store
- Officer No1
- Officer No2
- Guard Room
- Prison Cell
- Officers Kitchen
- Master Gunner
- Dormitory for 17 men
- Dormitory 2 rooms for 9 men each
- Cook House

Shoreham Fort

> Work had to stop due to the cold weather in the winter but Shoreham Fort was completed in six working months!
> Fort Nelson took 10 years and had 4 million bricks...

The Officers and Master Gunner had separate accommodation from the men, both ranks sharing a kitchen. The Master Gunner was the only paid personnel at Shoreham Fort and would have private quarters and, if married, would usually have his family living with him too, a fact indicated in the censuses of the time.

There were three rooms for accommodating the other ranks, with an adjoining cook house at the eastern end of the barrack block which contained a large range cooker. Supplies for the kitchens would have been kept in the barrack store at the western end of the barrack block. This was next to the artillery store which housed the rifles and tools for the cannons.

Initially built to accommodate 2 Officers, 1 Master Gunner and 48 NCO's (Non-Commissioned Officers) and Privates, a general report on sanitary conditions in 1860 advised that the space available was not acceptable, so the number of NCO's and Privates was reduced to 35.

The fort required up to 300 soldiers to man it during an attack, the barrack block itself housing enough to operate the cannons. By keeping the enemy far enough out to sea it meant the rest of the soldiers could make their way over the river by ferry or possibly walking across to Soldier's Point, at low tide.

The barrack block underwent modifications by the military and whilst it was a private residence. Demolished in 1958, by the Local Authority, Shoreham Fort was lucky in so much as the barrack block was taken down due to being a residential area. Littlehampton Fort, on the other hand, saw its barrack block filled with explosives and blown up - destroying many other areas of the fort too.

When exposing the barrack block foundations at Shoreham, it became apparent that areas matched no previously seen plans. Further research clarified WWII modifications incorporated a gas decontamination centre.

A Hidden History

Shoreham Fort

Carnot Wall

Shoreham Fort's carnot wall, at its original height, stood 12ft tall and allowed the soldiers to stand behind, aiming their rifles through the rifle loops (windows in the wall). With an unexpected ditch and a sheer drop of 15ft, our soldiers had the advantage of surprise.

The wall was built with Portland Stone, red brick from local brick works and Sussex beach flints, of which there was an infinite supply. Keeping materials locally sourced reduced both the cost and time to build the fort.

Littlehampton Fort

Shoreham Fort's wall has a rounded top making it very difficult for the enemy to grip if they got close enough to try and climb over it. Littlehampton has a completely different finish as it is triangulated.

As Shoreham's wall is not visible from the sea any invaders would have been ill prepared and would not have had any equipment to help them scale it.

Have you noticed how many of the words used in the fortification designs are French..? Caponier means 'Chicken House'!

Lazare Carnot (1753-1823)

The carnot wall is a loop-holed wall built in the ditch of a fort and takes its name from the French mathematician, politician and military engineer, Lazare Carnot. His ideas on fortifications were published in 1810 under the title 'Traite de la Défense des Places Fortes'. The English Translation, 'A Treatise on the Defence of Fortified Places', was published in 1814.

Shoreham Fort

Caponiers

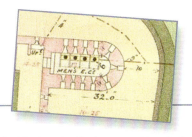

A caponier is a roofed stronghold protecting the ditch outside of the carnot wall. Bastions were used before caponiers and were a projecting horseshoe shape incorporated in the carnot wall, allowing soldiers to fire along the outer ditch.

The soldiers would stand behind each rifle loop, making it almost impossible for the attacking force to get a clear shot. The loops were designed to minimise the noise and stop smoke from the guns infiltrating the inside of the caponier, as was the height and pitch of the roof.

The east and west caponiers served an addition purpose: They were the toilets! The west was used by the officers and the east by the other men. In the east caponier there is evidence of where slate divides once were, providing the soldiers with some privacy.

Littlehampton Fort

Hurst Castle

Bastions would have been useless at Shoreham Fort. They would offer the soldiers absolutely no protection from incoming enemy fire or ricocheting shingle from the beach, if the enemy shot fell short.

Shoreham Fort's caponiers are situated on the south, east and west faces of the fort. The strategic locations giving the men inside a full view along the entire carnot wall, ditch and up onto the beach.

Caponiers were also used to add to the defences of older structures. Hurst Castle, Lymington, is a prime example of an addition being made to a structure built by Henry VIII.

Shoreham Fort is unique due to the carnot wall and caponier combination. It is now the last fort of its kind in the country, maybe the world, that has both incorporated in its design.

A Hidden History

Magazines

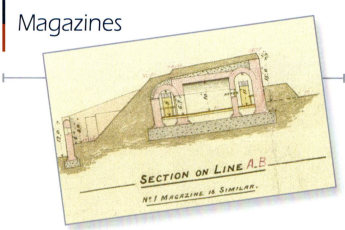

> The word magazine comes from the Arabic word 'makhazin' which means storehouse or warehouse.

At the east and west end of the fortification are two magazines. These consist of chambers with arched roofs to give them strength. Above these chambers earth was built up to a thickness of over 5ft to absorb any direct hit from enemy cannon shot.

Gunpowder needs to be stored in dry conditions as damp powder would cause cannons and rifles to misfire. The Victorians knew that to keep a room dry, it needed to 'breath'. Consequently, the magazines are built with cavity walls and air vents.

Each magazine originally comprised of store and shifting room where the shells and gunpowder were kept. Both magazines were designed to hold one hundred and twenty six barrels of gunpowder each. The west magazine included a laboratory area where the gunpowder would be mixed or made into charges before being stored. When needed the charges and shells would be moved to the shell recesses.

The magazines were not lit but having lime washed walls meant it would help to brighten the area. In later forts lighting passages were integrated in the design. Oil lamps, behind glass, were then lit ensuring no naked flames were in the vicinity of the gunpowder.

Between 1857 and 1886 the west magazine was modified to incorporate a third smaller room. The room was known as a lobby and was the area for the soldiers to change from their uniform and hobnail boots, into lab coats and leather slippers, to prevent a spark causing and explosion.

The implementation of the above designs highlights that health and safety was an important factor to the Victorians.

Shoreham Fort

Shell Recesses

A Powder Monkey wore white gloves as part of his uniform, this was to indicate whether a gunpowder bag had split. Any broken bags would not be issues to the men above, potentially saving lives - if powder was issued at a lower charge it could be very dangerous for the crews firing the cannon, another health and safety measure.

Shell recesses were a new development as part of the prototype fortification.

The shell recesses are under the terreplein and gun emplacements and were kept supplied from the magazines. Their purpose was temporary storage for the shells and gunpowder, making them closer to the cannons. This allowed quicker reloading of the cannons without having to walk to the magazines.

Shoreham Fort has three shell recesses shared between its six cannons, one for each pair. The doors of the Shell recesses were solid wood to keep the powder safe and dry when not in use.

The shells would be handed up to the gun crews on the steps above by young cadets, also known as 'Powder Monkeys'. These young Powder Monkeys were about sixteen years of age.

By using a sixteen year old boy it potentially meant that the next generation of gunner was already working at the fort. At eighteen he could step up to become gun crew. His previous knowledge and understanding of fort life giving him an advantage over new recruits.

The shell recesses at Shoreham Fort are built at ground level, the same level as the magazines, making access easier. Littlehampton Fort's shell recesses were built up next to the guns, making them less accessible and causing the Powder Monkey to run further.

Shoreham Fort's recesses tell their own story. They show signs of target practice use in WWI as they are peppered with holes from the .303 rounds fired from the Short Magazine Lee Enfield, this could have been the H Company of the Royal Sussex Regiment when they were stationed there.

A Hidden History

Artillery

Shoreham Fort was designed with six gun emplacements positioned about 15ft above sea level, Littlehampton only having five. The increased visibility over the harbour entrance and neighbouring beaches, in turn increased the defence of the fort. In front of the gun emplacements, facing the sea, is a high grassy bank known as a rampart. The rampart hid the cannons from any ships approaching the harbour - all that could be seen was grass, not the emplacements behind it.

Gun emplacements were built for the cannons to traverse on, they also played a part in protecting the cannon and crew due to the specifically shaped earth mounds built on each side.

Upon completion the fort was armed with six smooth bore 68-pounder cannons that were later replaced by rifled Palliser conversions given two 64- pounder RML (rifled muzzle loader) and four 32-pounder RML. The 32-pounder cannons were replaced giving the fort four 64-pounder and two 80-pounders cannons. A later addition to the fort was a 40-pounder breech loading cannon, as used on HMS Warrior, this was later incorporated into an artillery train.

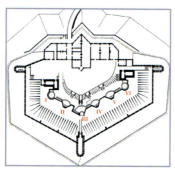

Each cannon stood on large wooden carriages that were placed on the pivot and rails. The cannons would be pulled into position by the men using a block and tackle system, along with the iron loops that were built into the side of the gun emplacement wall. Seven to eight men would be needed to crew each cannon due to the sheer size and weight of the artillery piece.

ARMAMENT	
NATURE OF PIECES	Nº
64 Pᴿ. R.M.L. 58 Cᵂᵀ.	3
80 Pᴿ. R.M.L. 5 TONS.	2
TOTAL	5

Shoreham Fort

The Palliser conversion was designed in 1863 by Major Sir William Palliser CB, MP (captain at time of invention). The purpose of his design was to update old but serviceable muzzle loading cannons. To implement the new design the inside of a barrel was sleeved creating a rifled bore. This made a shell spin when fired - dramatically increasing the accuracy and distance.

A Palliser conversion was a much cheaper alternative to the new rifled Armstrong Guns that had starting to be produced. They were also much lighter and more manoeuvrable too.

All of Shoreham's cannons were upgraded using this technique, keeping the fort up to date with current technology.

MAJOR SIR WILLIAM PALLISER, C.B., M.P. (ARTILLERIST)
Died Jan. 4, Aged 51

> Who'd have thought that one extra cannon could make so much difference to the fire power at Shoreham...
> By the time Shoreham had fired all six cannons, Littlehampton had only fired three because Shoreham fired in pairs.

A Hidden History

Prototypes & Comparisons

Prototypes for the Palmerston Forts
Littlehampton Fort was completed in 1854 before Lord Palmerston became prime minister.

Newhaven Lunette was built 1855 but is not a complete fort. Work stopped to save money and resources to build Newhaven Fort on the top of Castle Hill, the higher location giving an advantage to the distance the cannons could fire and the crews could see.

Shoreham Fort was built 1857 rectifying design flaws in the first two prototypes learning, in some cases, to progress from what could have been fatal errors.

As Newhaven Lunette was a battery, Littlehampton Fort and Shoreham Fort are used as comparisons.

Artillery
The extra cannon enabled the Master Gunner to fire the cannons in pairs, this doubled Shoreham's rate of fire power as by the time Shoreham had fired all six cannons, Littlehampton had only fired three. With an asymmetrical design at Shoreham Fort it enabled four cannons to defend the harbour, which was the main objective. With the two end cannons, being able to fire a full 360 degrees, it meant the fort was defended on all sides and could protect the shores from Brighton to Worthing, including the port and river behind. This range was possible because of the rifled conversions which were not installed at Littlehampton.

The cannons at Shoreham Fort were still in situ through WWI and up to WWII. Unfortunately, the cannons at Littlehampton Fort could not be fired: The Fortification 'Provisions of Expense' Bill from August 1860 states that the fort was 'built on boggy foundations, and the whole structure is now so insecure that the guns could not be fired if wanted.' Consequently, the cannons were removed thirty one years later in 1891.

Bastions & Caponiers
Around the outside walls of the forts were defensible areas which allowed the soldiers to fire their rifles along the ditch; bastions at Littlehampton and roofed caponiers at Shoreham. Littlehampton's bastions were situated in such a way that, if used, the soldiers would be shooting at each other. The positioning was corrected at Shoreham with the caponiers being situated at the most northern points of the east and west walls.

Coal Cellar
At Shoreham Fort the coal cellar was built on the outside of the fort in the Banquette rather than inside the fort, as seen at Littlehampton Fort. This was so that deliveries could be made without breaching the security of the fort.

Magazines
The additional lobby, that was introduced as a safety measure, in Shoreham Fort's west magazine was never added to Littlehampton Fort but was an essential feature of forts thereafter. The soldiers at Littlehampton had a cut out arch of brick, similar to a shell recess, on the external north wall of the west magazine. This meant that they were open to the elements when making charges and at risk of the powder getting wet or being blown away.

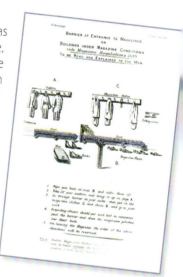

Shoreham Fort

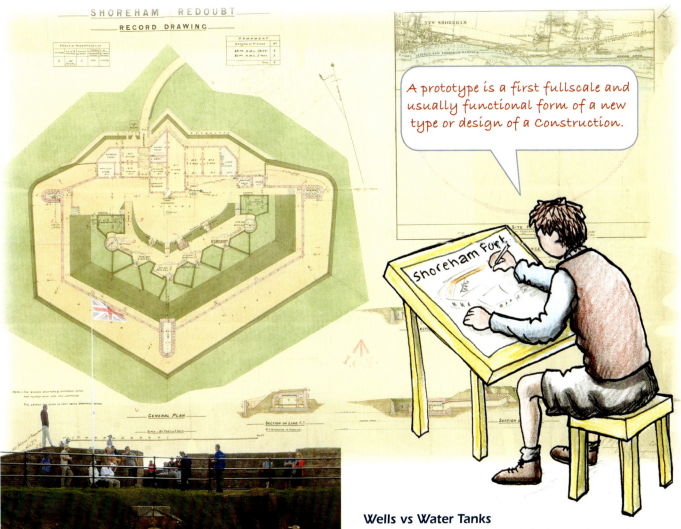

A prototype is a first fullscale and usually functional form of a new type or design of a Construction.

Slopes and Steps
Littlehampton had two sets of steps but a slope was installed at Shoreham Fort to give easier access to the terreplein and gun emplacements from the parade ground. This enabled the soldiers to use rollers to move the barrels of the cannon up top, rather than having to lift a great deal of weight up steps.

Wells vs Water Tanks
Littlehampton Fort's water wells, being so close to the sea, would turn brackish (salty) at high tide. Within six months of moving in most of the soldiers had come down with dysentery. Shoreham Fort was built with two water tanks under the parade ground. These held 11,578 gallons of water, which was collected from the flat roofs of the barrack block. The water was pumped in such a way that both tanks were kept moving and could not stagnate. A filtration pump may have also been used to further filter the water. This was mentioned in the 1860's report on sanitary conditions. Littlehampton was modified at a later date to incorporate tanks, two being above ground.

A Hidden History

1st Sussex Artillery Volunteers

Shoreham Fort was manned by the 1st Sussex Artillery Volunteers from 1859. Between 1857 and 1859 it was manned by the militia.

The 1st Sussex Artillery Volunteers were considered to be foremost among Volunteer Artillery units. In 1865, at the Shoeburyness National Artillery Meeting, they won the Queen's Prize and the Lord Palmerston Prize for accurate shooting. In 1896 while demonstrating an armoured train they achieved "excellent practice" with a 40-pounder cannon; the train was deployed along the coastline between Newhaven and Shoreham. In the army list of 1896 Sussex is listed as forth of sixty two in "Order of Procedure of the several counties in the volunteer Artillery Force".

For local competitions, prize giving ceremonies were held in places like Brighton Pavilion and Shoreham's Swiss Gardens. They were very grand occasions.

The photograph shows the 1st Sussex Artillery Volunteers at Shoreham Fort wearing a typical uniform of the time. The picture was taken in 1897 for Queen Victoria's Diamond Jubilee. The blue helmet has a distinctive badge plate which was specific to the 1st Sussex Artillery Volunteers. Officers wore a cross belt, waist belt with sword sling and sword; their knots being silver. Other ranks are seen parading with waist belts and Martini Henry rifles, their tunic and trousers are dark blue serge. There is red piping on the tunic and red stand up collars. Buttons, belts and helmet plates are silver. None of the Volunteers were paid, apart from the Master Gunner, and they all had to buy their own uniform. This of course encouraged them to look after it and use it regularly. The 1st Sussex Artillery Volunteer's recruitment office was 43 High Street, Shoreham, next to the old Town Hall.

Shoreham Fort was disbanded, no longer used for military purpose, in 1906, but Kelly's Directory shows the recruitment office still in use until 1911, albeit changing to Territorial Force, Sub Section of 3rd Sussex Battery 1st home Counties Brigade of the Royal Field Artillery.

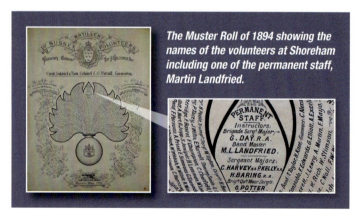

The Muster Roll of 1894 showing the names of the volunteers at Shoreham including one of the permanent staff, Martin Landfried.

Shoreham Fort

Shoreham Fort
A Hidden History | Activity Pages

Can you colour these pages to finish the brochure?

A Hidden History

Shoreham Fort
A Hidden History | Activity Pages

A soldier of the 1st Sussex Artillery Volunteers based at Shoreham.

Colour him in, cut him out and stand him up! (Please note, not suitable for paints)

This picture shows you the correct colours to use.

Fold along the dotted line and then glue narrow tab to the back of the soldier

Cut along this bottom edge and then around the rest of the soldier.

Shoreham Fort

Can you find the answers to the clues below?

Across
- 5 - Started the film studio at the fort (page 20) 9
- 6 - Name of building soldiers lived in (page 6) 7, 5
- 8 - Built in Shoreham Harbour during WWI (page 23) 7, 6
- 13 - Who designed something in 1863 (page 13) 8
- 14 - Monarch in 1897 when photo of soldiers was taken (page 16) 5, 8
- 15 - Number of shelf recesses at Shoreham Fort (page 11) 5
- 16 - Round defensive building with one cannon on top (page 4) 8, 5
- 17 - Shaped like a horseshoe (page 9) 7
- 18 - Shop one of the soldiers worked in (page17) 11
- 19 - Surname of identity bracelet owner (page 32) 5

Down
- 1 - Name of steam engine that carried a cannon (page 18) 8
- 2 - Name of character throughout the book 4
- 3 - Stored in the magazines (page 10) 3, 6
- 4 - British Prime Minister when Shoreham Fort was built (page 2) 10
- 7 - Which prototype in this book was built first (page 1) 13
- 9 - Where did Shoreham Fort's 6" guns come from originally (page 24) 11
- 10 - Who was wall named after (page 8) 6
- 11 - Napoleon III's boat (page 3) 2, 6
- 12 - First name of inventor of Nissen huts (page 31) 5

A Hidden History

This brochure has been completed by..

Shoreham Fort Wordsearch

C	J	I	B	U	T	L	I	N	S	E	O
A	H	O	U	P	R	I	V	A	E	M	C
P	F	O	R	T	O	A	N	T	M	A	B
O	S	L	S	E	R	U	M	J	A	O	U
N	R	H	A	R	H	E	G	P	G	N	L
I	E	C	A	R	N	O	T	W	A	L	L
E	T	L	T	E	C	B	A	Y	Z	R	E
R	S	T	O	P	I	H	R	P	I	Y	T
Y	A	N	A	L	K	C	A	N	N	O	N
U	D	E	L	E	R	A	Y	E	E	Z	K
S	O	L	D	I	E	R	V	T	A	E	S
R	P	N	M	N	C	I	R	I	F	L	E

Can you find these words?

Soldier - Cannon - Carponier - Carnot Wall - Fort
Rampart - Terreplein - Magazine - Rifle - Bullet

What did you like about Shoreham Fort the most?

Can you draw it on Jack's drawing board?

Across
5 Lyndhurst
6 Barrack Block
8 Mystery Towers
13 Palliser
14 Queen Victoria
15 Three
16 Martello Tower
17 Bastion
18 Hanningtons
19 Simon

Down
1 Goldsmid
2 Jack
3 Gun Powder
4 Palmerston
7 Littlehampton
9 Battleships
10 Carnot
11 La Gloire
12 Peter

< Crossword Answers

Shoreham Fort

When I am a little older I will have a uniform like this one, its got solid silver buttons you know. This one is my Dad's... Shhh, don't tell him...

Shoreham Fort's Artillery Volunteers

Band Master Martin Leonard Landfried 1834-1902
Martin Landfried was the Band Master of 1st Sussex Artillery Volunteers. He was also renowned internationally as the man who sounded the bugle for the 'Charge of the Light Brigade' at the battle of Balaclava, 25th October 1854. Landfried left the army in 1865, moved to Sussex and took a job in Hannington's department store, Brighton. Hanningtons was owned by Charles Smith Hannington; he was highly committed to the Volunteer movement and took command as Lieutenant Colonel in 1868. Martin joined the Volunteers in 1865, served for over thirty years, becoming bandmaster in 1890. Martin was injured in Balaclava and to raise money for fellow veterans he toured England playing his bugle in Music Halls.

A recording made of Martin playing the famous charge was distributed by the Light Brigade Relief Fund. The aim was to benefit the remaining veterans and inform the public about the bad times some of them had fallen on. This recording was made by Edison with his new wax cylinder technology at Edison House, Northumberland Avenue, London. Copies of this recording can still be heard today. Martin married his first wife Josephine Barnes, in 1866 and they had seven children, one of whom died in infancy. Josephine passed away in 1890 and Martin married Annie Knight. Martin died on 8th December 1902 at his home in Portland Road, Hove and was buried in Hove Cemetery on 13th December, with military honours.

In May 1894 Martin was at Tide Mills entertaining the dignitaries, with his bugle, at the testing of the armoured train before it headed for Sheffield Park.

William 'Albert' Collins 1877-1966
Albert was a volunteer at Shoreham Fort and was recorded describing his time there.

What a glorious time we 'ad. Our dress was exactly like the Royal Artillery. Never had no khaki. Our captain was Mister George Dell of Shoreham. Everyone got on with him. He always used to take us out, march out smoking concerts we 'ad. It was jolly good. That was when the beer was good - and every year we used to have the artillery practice and rifle shooting over the fort [at] Kingston. We used to have big gun drills. The targets used to be on a big tub in the open sea, but we didn't dare hit it, but get close to it 'cos 'twould do a lot of damage to the tubs.

Albert married Emily Ada Trims in 1902 and they had 6 children. In 1911 the family lived in the Duke of Wellington Public House, Shoreham and Albert was a yacht's blacksmith and licensed victualler. Albert later became a foreman at Lancing Carriage words, retiring at 70. This position seems quite fitting as he was part of the crew of the Artillery Train when they tested it at Sheffield Park in 1894.

One year we went to Lord Sheffield's place Sheffield Park, in the armoured train and er.. in the afternoon, no, in the morning rather, they was having practice at Newhaven and they brought the armoured train to Sheffield Park where we was and they was having a practice with the guns - at Sheffield. And one of the chaps put a live shell in the guns and as he was putting it in, one of the chaps notice him says "Take it out you fool! that's one of them live shells what they been practicing with in Newhaven for the targets!"

A Hidden History

M class 0-6-0ST 'Bradford'

LB&SC Railway
- Armoured Artillery Train *by Peter Briggs*

An armoured train was first suggested back in 1860 by a Mr Anderson who believed that guns mounted on railway rolling stock would give greater mobility. However, large guns mounted in this way present a big problem with recoil. If they were fired at 90 degrees to the track the recoil would simply 'push' the gun off the other side of the train! The recoil problem was overcome however in 1894 when Captain F. G. Stone of the Royal Artillery requested that an armoured train be built to patrol and protect the Sussex coast. It would be built by the London Brighton & South Coast Railway (LB&SCR) and carry a 40lb breech-loading Armstrong Gun borrowed from Shoreham Fort. Finances for this project came in the form of a contribution from Colonel General Goldsmid and Colonel Gervais Boxall.

Model made by Peter Briggs

The 40lb breech-loading Armstrong gun was mounted on a modified 4 wheel 20 ton machinery truck No. 7144 and could be turned though 360 degrees by the crew using wooden poles inserted into a capstan to rotate the mounting platform.

D3 class 0-4-4T No. 363 'Goldsmid'

The design was carried out by Mr Robert J. Billington assisted by Colonel Pollock of the Royal Artillery. Mr Billington was employed by the LB&SCR at that time and was a well-respected designer of steam locomotives. Many of the Officers and men of the 1st Sussex Volunteer Reserve force also worked for the LB&SCR and it was these men that would be responsible for the manning of the completed armoured train.

A shield was built around the gun with a vertical slot for the barrel to protrude through. Stability to counter the recoil was achieved by positioning the gun on ramps with a hydraulic damper fixed at the front and extending four retractable arms outwards. Adjustable feet attached at the end of these arms were then lowered to the ground. With all four feet firmly on the ground the truck was also clamped and wedged onto the rails.

Shoreham Fort

> The soldiers were all volunteers which meant that they had paid job to do as well. Some of the soldiers actually worked for the London Brighton & South Coast Railway

Two third class carriages were also armoured with iron plating; one to carry the ammunition and the other the gun crew. The carriage carrying the gun crew had a steel parapet with cut-outs so that soldiers could if necessary use their rifles to protect themselves and the train. The train was hauled by a D3 class 0-4-4T locomotive also designed by Robert J. Billington and built at the LB&SCR works.

The first trials took place on Saturday May 19th 1894 near the village of Tide Mills about 1.2miles south east of Newhaven. Sir Julian Goldsmid MP, the commanding officer of the Sussex Volunteer force, arranged the event for members of the Cabinet and War Office. On this particular day the train was hauled by the D3 class 0-4-4T No. 363 'Goldsmid'.

The gun was fired several times at a target moored in Seaford Bay with some success and eventually the target was destroyed. The design of the armoured truck showed that it was indeed possible to use a heavy gun on the railway successfully without the earlier problems encountered with the recoil.

The initial idea of the Armoured Train was to have at least three running on special tracks between Littlehampton & Brighton, Newhaven & Seaford and Pevensey & Hastings.

Despite the successful trials these tracks were never built but the train was in operation until the very late 1890's. It was hauled by the D3 class 0-4-4T No. 363 'Goldsmid' from 1894 – 1896 and then for two more years by the D3 class 0-4-4T No. 375 'Glynde'. In 1898 it was also seen being hauled by the Manning Wardle & Co. M class 0-6-0ST 'Bradford' owned by the Newhaven Harbour Company.

Picture provided by Trevor Povey

Film Studio

By the end of the 19th Century, moving film had been invented. One of the first cameras was patented by Thomas Edison in the early 1890's. Edison had also developed and improved wax recording methods and on 2nd August 1890, he used this new technology to record Martin Leonard Landfried, a veteran of the Crimean War and Volunteer at Shoreham Fort.

Francis Lyndhurst, grandfather of British actor Nicholas Lyndhurst, was a scenic artist who painted elaborate backdrops onto canvas for the theatre. Francis' knowledge of the theatre, his interest in the newly developed camera equipment and his attraction to the strong, natural light of the South Coast of England led him to establish his first film studio at Shoreham Fort.

The fort's location was perfect; the high walls of barrack block; the ramparts of the fort and the high magazines gave protections against the wind, thus reducing the ripple effect of the canvas which would ruin a scene. The fort also provided more than adequate security for the film studio within its protective perimeter walls.

Along with comic actor Will Evans, the Sunny South Film Company was formed and one of its best known films, shot at Shoreham Fort, was 'A Showman's Dream'.

Although Sunny South didn't last long, Francis' interest continued with Sealight Film Processing Company Ltd in 1915. It was whilst running this company that the Glasshouse Studio at the other end of the beach, close to the Church of the Good Shepherd, was built.

With the start of WWI Lyndhurst's German ancestry became an issue. Horatio Bottomley MP and creator of the John Bull magazine insisted that the concrete foundation, for the film studio, was in fact a gun emplacement for the Germans to use against Shoreham's Army Camp. In October 1914 the magazine cover boasted that its circulation was the largest of any weekly journal in the world. True or not it certainly provided Bottomley with a very influential outlet for his political and financial opinions.

Add to this propaganda the fact that the country was now funding a war effort, luxury industries, such as filming, lost their revenue streams. Sealight went bust and Francis returned to London and continued as a successful set designer.

Francis sold the Glasshouse Studio to Olympic Kine Trading Company but it appears not to have been used for making films. It was then sold in 1918 to Sidney Morgan, father of actress Joan Morgan, and his Progress Film Company used it to produce films over a four year period. Unfortunately filming had taken off in California by then but it has been said that if it wasn't for WWI, Shoreham may have become the centre of the motion picture industry and could have become Hollywood by Sea.

Some film studio buildings were destroyed in a fire late 1922 but the Glasshouse Studio remained until the early 1950's. It was used as a timber yard and when the bungalow next door caught fire the studio's fate was sealed; it burnt to the ground in front of a crowd of onlookers.

Shoreham Fort was once again used in 1958 when 'The Battle of the V1' was filmed there and other locations in the vicinity.

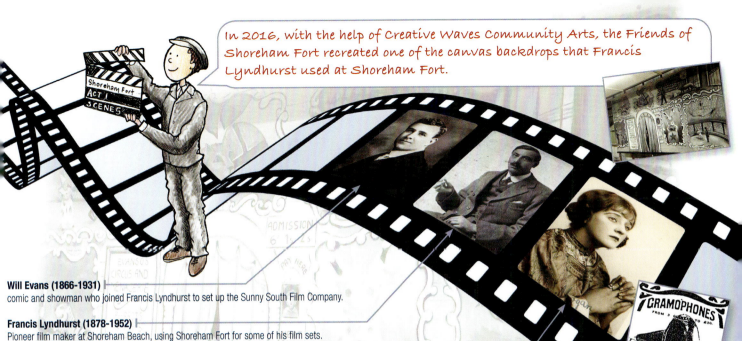

In 2016, with the help of Creative Waves Community Arts, the Friends of Shoreham Fort recreated one of the canvas backdrops that Francis Lyndhurst used at Shoreham Fort.

Will Evans (1866-1931)
comic and showman who joined Francis Lyndhurst to set up the Sunny South Film Company.

Francis Lyndhurst (1878-1952)
Pioneer film maker at Shoreham Beach, using Shoreham Fort for some of his film sets.

Joan Morgan (1905-2004)
starred in films at the Shoreham studio when it was run by her father, the film director, Sydney Morgan.

The Glasshouse Studio

Sealight Film Processing Company Ltd and Progress Film Company used the pure natural light of the Glasshouse Studio to make many early silent movies including Little Dorrit, A Lowland Cinderella and The Mayor of Casterbridge, to name just a few of the most well known titles.

The studio was used by Walter West Productions in 1922-23 for the production of a couple more films before Progress finally sold most of the site back to Mrs Easter in the late 1920's - Francis Lyndhurst having made the initial purchase from Mrs Easter in 1915.

Bungalow Town

Bungalow Town was the name given to Shoreham Beach in the early 1900's. It had the reputation of being a very bohemian place with theatre stars, actors and producers taking a liking to the area. Among national stars drawn to the area were Marie Loftus, music hall star and Will Evans, acrobat and comedian, plus many others who desired to have weekend, or holiday, homes by the sea. Many of the constructions were made from railway carriages. Two were placed either side of a concrete base and, with a roof constructed over the top, they had a very cheap home. Unfortunately WWII saw a majority of these bungalows destroyed by the British Army.

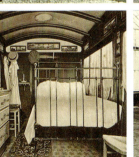

A Hidden History

Shoreham Camp from the air

The Great War

In all honesty, not much is known about Shoreham Fort in WWI, but it is well documented that the surrounding areas were of great importance to the war effort.

Shoreham Fort was used for military training and storage purposes and the Friends of Shoreham Fort, who are continuously researching this era of the fort's history, came across a reference to a WWI diary for the Royal Sussex Regiment which confirmed the regiment's use of the fort.

The enlistment of men to Kitchener's new army posed an immediate problem - accommodation of all the extra soldiers. Billeting on civilians was a temporary answer, the long-term solution was the construction of new camps. Under the terms of DORA, Defence of the Realm Act, 1914, the War Office could requisition land. One of the first sites acquired was the Southdown Golf Club on Slonk Hill, at the top of Shoreham – the club received £182 compensation for the land. From Slonk Hill the camp spread down to Buckingham House, a private residence then owned by William Godson Little.

Shoreham Camp was part of large camp which spread across the Downs from Worthing to Portslade. One of Shoreham's roles, in preparing soldiers heading to France, was to train them in the art of trench building but this wasn't a true reflection of the conditions the soldier would be forced to endure. Shoreham Downs were chalk whereas many of the battlefields of France were mud. The chalk aided the drainage of rain water and the trenches here were drier, unlike those abroad.

On 12th September 1914 H Company of the Royal Sussex Regiment, who were stationed at Canterbury, were "ordered to proceed to Shoreham and get a camp ready for the newly formed Division of what is usually called Kitchener's Army."

On 21st September 1914 "H Coy returned from Shoreham and went into quarters at the Fort, and the lines of tents were shifted lower down the hill and rather further away from the road."

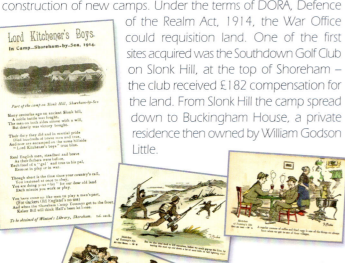

East and West Camp at Shoreham started as tented sites and the foul weather during the winter of 1914-15 turned the ground into a quagmire. The men had to be moved out to billets in Shoreham, Worthing, Southwick and Portslade. Troops returned to the camps when wooden huts, built by Robert McAlpine & Sons, were installed to house them.

It wasn't only Shoreham that had a specific role in training the soldiers, Portslade had the Army School of Cookery and Southwick, on The Green, had the Royal Marine Engineers who were responsible for building the Mystery Towers in Shoreham Harbour.

Towards the end of the war that two strange looking towers were built in the harbour. They created a lot interest and much speculation as to what they were for but naturally, being wartime, the whole building programme was a military secret.

Once the war was over the significance of these structures was revealed. The intention was for sixteen towers to be built. They were to be towed into position in the English Channel and sunk in a line stretching from Dungeness to Cap Gris Nez, France - the nearest point to England. Boom nets were to be strung between each tower to stop the German U-boats passing through the Channel.

These super structures were supposed to be a fantastic defence. Instead they ended up being an embarrassment to the government, due to their huge costs. Of the two towers completed one was towed out of the harbour, 12th September 1920, to the waters off the Isle of Wight and is the Nab Tower Lighthouse. The second was finally dismantled and sections can still be found in several pathways around Southwick.

Many of the Royal Sussex soldiers, billeted at Shoreham Fort during WWI, would not have returned home after the war. The Regiment suffered terribly on one particular day, 30th June 1916 and this day has become known locally as 'The Day Sussex Died'.

The Battle of the Boar's Head, Richebourg l'Avoue, was planned as a diversionary tactic to make the German Command believe that this area of the Pas de Calais was the one chosen for the major offensive of 1916. The intention was to prevent the Germans from moving troops to the Somme area, some fifty kilometres to the south.

Mention Richebourg and many will give an unknowing look, yet Richebourg played a significant role in the Battle of the Somme and The Royal Sussex Regiment's history.

On June 23rd news was received that there was to be an attack on the Boar's Head, a salient of the German lines. The battalions only had days, not weeks, to prepare, with initial instructions given that the 11th Battalion should lead the attack with the 12th on their right and the 13th in reserve. The roles of the 11th and 13th were reversed at the last minute.

At 3:05am the Battle of the Boar's Head commenced and lasted less than five hours.

Between the 3 Southdown Battalions 17 officers and 349 men were killed. Over 1,000 were wounded or taken prisoner and the 13th Battalion was all but wiped out.

We found a soldier's diary in the archives and in that diary it told us that 100 Royal Sussex soldiers were living at the fort during WW1.

A Hidden History

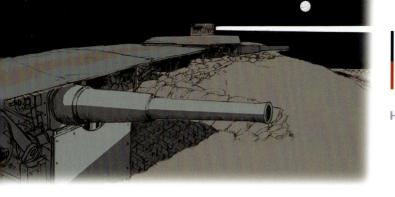

The Second World War

During WWII the port of Shoreham played a huge part in supplying troops, landing craft and supplies to our front lines abroad. Shoreham Fort was extensively modified to defend the harbour and to guard against possible invasion. Two large ammunition stores were built on top of the terreplein and the ancient gun emplacements were modified to accept two 6in naval guns. These guns had been used on battleships during WW1 but were recycled in 1939 as coastal defence guns.

An aiming light station was built at the east end of the fort with its counterpart about five bungalows to the west and an observation tower was built on top of the west magazine. This tower and the south caponier both had 'throw' switches installed so that, when armed, they could activate live mines. These mines were to be used to blow up the harbour entrance after the enemy had entered. Once their only exit was sealed, the two oil tanks in the grounds of Shoreham College would be emptied into the harbour and ignited.

Nissen huts were also erected to extend the barrack block accommodation for the servicemen, including Navy, Army regulars, members of the Royal Observer Corps (ROC) and the Home Guard.

Apart from the changes to the fort, there were drastic changes to the local landscape. The government was concerned that if there was a successful invasion the enemy would have ready made barracks for their men. Due to this a majority of the properties on Shoreham Beach were demolished to stop any invading forces from billeting their troops. A few houses survived as they were used for military purpose.

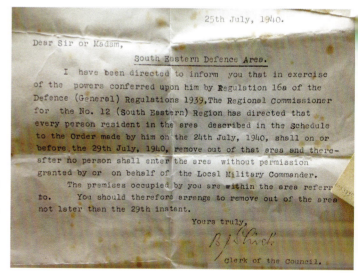

Beach residents were given very little notice to vacate their homes, some as little as 48 hours. Many, unable to remove all their personal belongings, had to leave things behind.

Shoreham Fort

This 1940's photo shows, despite everything being demolished, the Church of the Good Shepherd still standing. Story has it that the only reason it survived the threat of demolition is due to soldiers praying inside who refused to leave.

Being so close to Shoreham Airport, the fort had anti-aircraft guns installed in five locations around the fort's perimeter. Silhouettes of aircraft were used to instruct and train the Anti-Aircraft Gunners in accurate aircraft recognition. This was crucial to prevent mistaking friendly aircraft for the enemy. The training dome that was located at Shoreham Airport is still there today.

The aerial view of Shoreham Fort c1942 shows the extensive modifications undertaken to the fort itself.

Anti tank blocks were installed all the along the beach from Shoreham Fort towards Worthing Pier and beyond; wooden huts were added to the outskirts of the fort's boundary; blast walls were added in front of the barrack block and trenches were dug to increase defences, should the fort come under attack.

One record book for the fort during WWII shows how many small arms were assigned and the ammunition issued. It even states how the ration were allocated.

Shoreham Fort was responsible for letting Shoreham Airport know that enemy aircraft was on its way. There were 5 anti-aircraft guns added to the fort in WWII as well as two massive 6in guns which could fire more than 9 miles out to sea.

A Hidden History

Image provided by Trevor Povey

Fort Dwelling

A front door was cut through the north face of the building and the internal layout was changed to suit domestic needs.

Stephen Easter owned Shoreham Fort and The Langmaid family lived there. Members of the family have been back to visit the fort and through family photos and conversations much has been learned about the layout and uses of the fort at that time. One of the family was actually born in the fort on Christmas Day 1935. The family had to move out during the Second World War but were allowed to come back afterwards. They moved out permanently in the mid 1950's.

You can see from the pictures that, whilst used as a private residence, the barrack block had been rendered and some of the metal shuttering on the outside remained in place.

After being disbanded in 1906 there was no reason for the military to be at Shoreham Fort until the first world war started. A Harry Hunt was living at the fort in August 1915 and his attestation papers prove this. After the end of WWI it is believe that the fort lay empty for several years. It isn't until the 1920's that any detailed evidence of the family that spent many years living at Shoreham Fort comes to light.

In the mid 1920's a second floor was added onto the east wing of the Barrack Block and it became a house.

> Mr Langmaid used to have a motorbike and side car, as well as a Jaguar car. It looked amazing and fun to drive.

Shoreham Fort

1958 - The end of the Barrack Block

Purpose? or Decline and Decay?

Shoreham Fort was used for purposes other than military, such as the film studio & private dwelling. It was used by scout troops including Bethnal Green (shown in the photo) and Shipley who left evidence by way of pencilled graffiti in the west magazine. 1st Clapham Crusaders Troop also used the site and this is recorded in newspaper articles.

Once the fort stopped having a purpose it quickly fell into disrepair. Looking at photos from the Langmaid family's home and at a photo taken in 1977, showing the fort deserted, you realise how much damage can happen in a very short space of time. Therefore it needs to be ensured that history doesn't repeat itself.

Scouts at Shoreham Fort

1st Shipley Scouts were established in 1934

August 1913 - Bethnal Green scout group using the site for their summer camp.

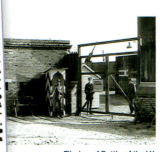

30th March 1910 - 1st Clapham Scouts

Filming of Battle of the V1

Fort used for Port Dumping Ground

1977

A Hidden History

1970's Restoration by Fred Aldsworth

The repairs and restoration undertaken in the period 1977-1979 had commenced the previous year with clearance and salvage works by 'volunteers' from various branches of the armed services under my supervision.

Foremost amongst these were trainees from HMS Daedalus, one of the primary shore airfields of the Fleet Air Arm, first established at Lee-on-the-Solent, Hampshire, as a seaplane base in 1917 and closed in 1999.

The volunteers camped on site and undertook a range of work which included the recovery of bricks for re-cycling. Associated with this was some mechanical clearance of the shingle in the surrounding ditch and the removal of overburden from the parade ground.

The next task was a detailed examination of the surviving structure and old photographs, including that of the 1st Sussex Artillery Volunteers in the 1890s, in order to determine the original form of the gun emplacements and to agree a strategy for reconstruction with English Heritage. This later benefited from the discovery of the 1886 survey in the Public Record Office and the discovery of water tanks under the parade ground. These led to the creation of a new plan of the fort.

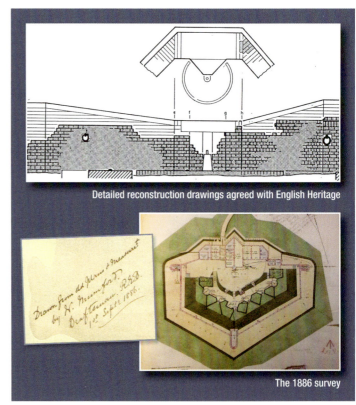

Detailed reconstruction drawings agreed with English Heritage

The 1886 survey

Shoreham Fort

Restoration commenced the following year and benefited from a scheme sponsored by West Sussex County Council, on behalf of the Manpower Services Commission - a non-departmental public body of the Department of the Employment Group created by Edward Heath's Conservative Government in 1973, through their Job Creation and Special Tempo-rary Employment Programmes.

This enabled the employment of a skilled bricklayer, Dennis Lord, a skilled flint worker, Paul Baker, and a support team to commence restoration of the gun emplacements, which were considered to be at the greatest threat of loss.

Large blocks of granite were acquired to replace those which originally formed the thresholds of the gun embrasures and new blocks of stone replaced those forming the corners of the steps which allowed the defenders to look and fire over the walls between them.

On completion of the six gun emplacements and three flights of steps, attention was turned to the south caponier, where vandals had broken through some of the rifle slits to gain entry into the interior. These were restored and then the openings fully blocked externally in an attempt to prevent further damage and entry.

Sections of the carnot wall were also restored where the pebble flint work had been either badly damaged or lost by erosion. Finally, some landscaping was undertaken; new rolled, shingled surfaces were laid on the parade ground and on the terreplein; and an information board was erected.

The terreplein and gun emplacements before and after restoration. Looking east.

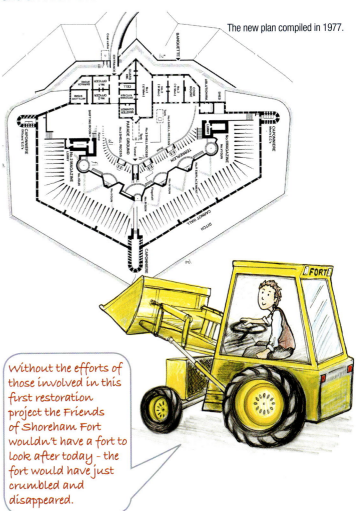

The new plan compiled in 1977.

Without the efforts of those involved in this first restoration project the Friends of Shoreham Fort wouldn't have a fort to look after today - the fort would have just crumbled and disappeared.

A Hidden History

Friends of Shoreham Fort

The Friends of Shoreham Fort (FOSF) was officially launched on 9th May 2010, by Gary Baines.

Gary first visited the fort with his Grandfather in 1984 when he was four years old. Sadly this is his only memory of his grandfather, as he passed away that same year. Gary started researching the fort at fourteen, setting up the first website in 1999, in an attempt to gain public support. The rest as they say is history...

In 2012 FOSF became a registered charity with the help of Sharon Penfold and Jackie Remfrey and it is the aim of the charity to "conserve, maintain and restore Shoreham Fort, a Scheduled Ancient Monument."

'Giving history a future, by bringing history to life'
- the charity motto.

Being the last fort of its kind that incorporates a carnot wall and caponier system, it is vital that this nationally significant heritage site is preserved for years to come, enabling us to promote the historical importance of the site. This is achieved through guided tours, presentations, school visits, living history displays and events, thus enhancing the site and literally bringing history to life.

Working with others we will promote our local history, such as Bungalow Town and the film industry. By also incorporating Buckingham Camp, mystery towers and coastal defences etc, Shoreham Fort will become a hub for military history too.

The FOSF are working towards a full restoration, where possible, including the reinstatement of the Barrack Block. This will enable the site to be used as a multi-purpose community facility. This in itself will give the fort a more permanent purpose and secure its future for many generations to come.

I really enjoy my time volunteering as a Friend of Shoreham Fort, it means that we get cake and fudge sometimes as a treat.

We are giving history a future...

Nissen Hut

For 56 years, two WWII land girls, Vera Barlow and Edith Hooper, lived in a Nissen hut situated on an acre of land in Chidham near Chichester, West Sussex. Both died in 2012, Vera, 87 and Edith, 92.

To raise enough money to live on, Vera and Edith kept pigs, did an egg round and washed dishes at a local hospital. When they died, the Nissen hut was in a very poor state. It was surrounded by overgrown vegetation and crumbling buildings including the pigs' sty and other Nissen hut bases.

This particular Nissen hut was used during WWII to accommodate the Canadian soldiers who were manning the anti-aircraft guns that were protecting the nearby harbour.

In 2013, Hayley Cropp, one of the Friends of Shoreham Fort, highlighted a news reports of a Nissen hut for sale. The FOSF's details were forwarded to the new owners who agreed to donate the hut to the charity. The hut was dismantled, moved and reassembled at Shoreham Fort, on one of the original Nissen hut bases laid down during WWII. It was realised during the rebuild that the hut had been assembled originally with parts dating from WWI. This was evident by the internal panels being different colours; blue from the Royal Flying Corps; green from the Army; brown from the Army Cater- ing Corps and white from the Army Medical corps. The design of the internal steel ribs has also been verified as WWI. This WWI Nissen hut was erected in the centenary years of that war.

Nissen Huts are named after their inventor – Peter Norman Nissen (1871-1930). When he invented them he was a Major in the British army, the 29th Company Royal Engineers. The huts were delivered on standard army lorries as a flat-pack kit, including a spanner. Being semi-circular there were no complicated eaves, gables or guttering and many of the parts such as the corrugated sheets were interchangeable. Apparently it was possible for four men to erect a hut in four hours...

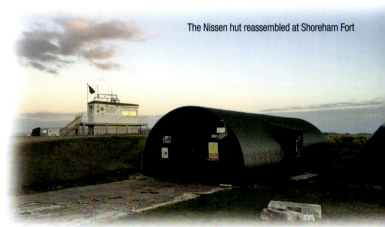

The Nissen hut reassembled at Shoreham Fort

Squirrelled Away… What is in Your Attic?

Many people don't realise what history they hold. Be it old postcards, letters, family photos, medals or other militaria. For example this photo, from the Langmaid family, showed a relative on a sidecar.

When you look at the photograph above properly it reveals so much more…

You can see the modifications to the walls to enable an entrance. You can see the magazine doors. You can see the flag pole position. Most importantly though, in the background is a cannon, still in its firing position… This photo was taken in 1938 proving that the fort was still armed until WWII.

This identity bracelet was found in 1988 on Shoreham Beach whilst a resident of a railway carriage bungalow was digging a fishpond in their garden. The identity of the bracelet was discovered by Andy Ramus in 2015 and the family of 2nd Lt Philip Frederick Howard Simon were traced. The family were contacted and they wanted the bracelet to stay in Shoreham and the beach resident kindly donated it to the Friends of Shoreham Fort. We'll never know how the bracelet was lost but we are incredibly grateful for the donation and for Andy's research.

With the closing of many military museums it is a sad fact that history is disappearing. Items, such as these, are being lost in house clearances etc. If you have items that you are unsure of their significance then please get in touch, if the Friends of Shoreham Fort don't have the answer, someone they know may be able to help.

Shoreham Fort